How the World Celebrates

Independence Days

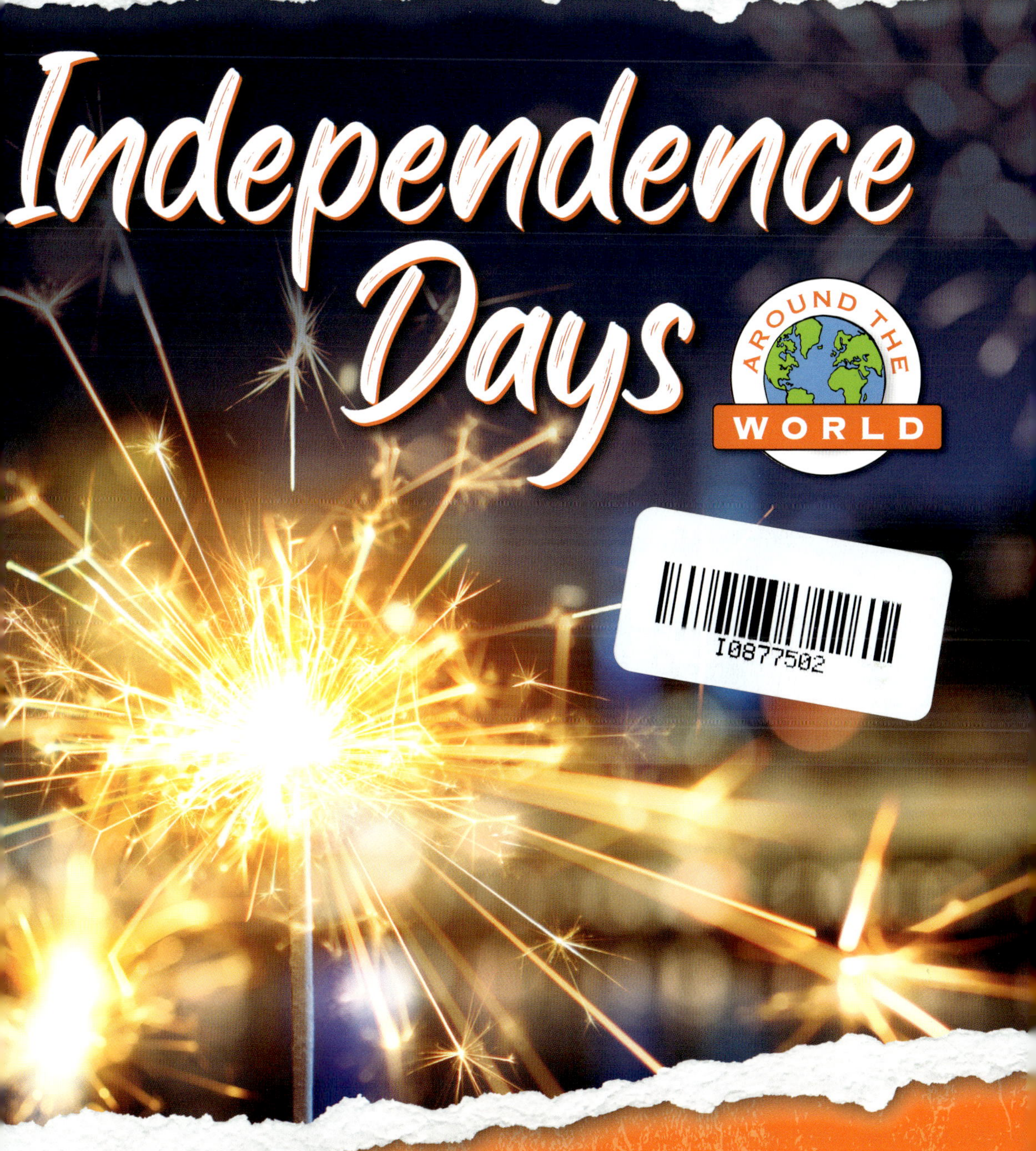

Around the World

Jennifer Kleiman

45TH PARALLEL PRESS

Published in the United States of America by Cherry Lake Publishing Group
Ann Arbor, Michigan
www.cherrylakepublishing.com

Reading Adviser: Beth Walker Gambro, MS, Ed., Reading Consultant, Yorkville, IL

Photo Credits: © phive/Shutterstock, cover, title page; © Aleksandar_Markov/Shutterstock, 4; © Charles Brutlag/Shutterstock, 6; © Kimberly's Impressions/Shutterstock, 8; © ShaikhMeraj/Shutterstock, 12; © neeraj_guptaa/Shutterstock, 14; © Rainbow_dazzle/Shutterstock, 15; © A 5/Shutterstock, 16; © ManaswiPatil/Shutterstock, 17; © Paul Weinberg via Wikimedia Commons CC BY-SA 3.0, 18; © Tatohra/Shutterstock, 20; © Schavda via Wikimedia Commons CC BY-SA 3.0, 21; © Lucian Coman/Shutterstock, 22; © IOIO IMAGES/Shutterstock, 23; © Muszynski Johann/Shutterstock, 24; © Marie-Lan Nguyen / Wikimedia Commons / CC-BY 2.5; © Dennis van de Water/Shutterstock, 28; © Alexandre.ROSA/Shutterstock, 29

45th Parallel Press is an imprint of Cherry Lake Publishing Group.

Library of Congress Cataloging-in-Publication Data

Names: Kleiman, Jennifer, 1978- author.
Title: Independence days around the world / written by Jennifer Kleiman.
Description: Ann Arbor, MI : 45th Parallel Press, 2025. | Series: How the world celebrates | Audience: Grades 4-6 | Summary: "Freedom rings in countries around the world. Readers will explore how different countries celebrate their independence, and the customs and traditions that define those celebrations. This hi-lo narrative nonfiction series celebrates diverse cultures while highlighting how expressions of joy and connection are all part of the human experience"-- Provided by publisher.
Identifiers: LCCN 2024036429 | ISBN 9781668956540 (hardcover) | ISBN 9781668957394 (paperback) | ISBN 9781668958261 (ebook) | ISBN 9781668959138 (pdf)
Subjects: LCSH: Fourth of July--Juvenile literature. | Independence Day (India)--Juvenile literature. | Freedom Day (South Africa)--Juvenile literature. | Bastille Day--Juvenile literature.
Classification: LCC E286 .A13838 2025 | DDC 973.3/6--dc23/eng/20240925
LC record available at https://lccn.loc.gov/2024036429

Cherry Lake Publishing would like to acknowledge the work of the Partnership for 21st Century Learning, a network of Battelle for Kids. Please visit Battelle for Kids online for more information.

Printed in the United States of America

NOTE FROM PUBLISHER: Websites change regularly, and their future contents are outside of our control. Supervise children when conducting any recommended online searches for extended learning opportunities.

Table of Contents

DID YOU KNOW? The Republic of San Marino is the world's oldest country. The nation was founded in 301 BCE. But its independence was not recognized until 1631. That's almost 2,000 years later!

Introduction

Independence. People work for it. They fight for it. They have even died for it. Once they have it, they celebrate it. What makes independence so important?

Independence means being free from outside control. An independent nation is free to make its own decisions. An independent nation is **sovereign**. It does not answer to another government. It can form independent relationships with other nations. It can trade with them. It can negotiate agreements. Its people can speak for themselves.

An independent nation is also free to form its own identity. It can promote its own culture.

Independence is worth celebrating. Every year, countries around the globe celebrate their independence. They **commemorate** it in meaningful ways. When you commemorate something, you remember it. You honor it.

The Declaration of Independence marks the birth of the United States of America.

THE HISTORY OF COLONIALISM

Empires have existed for thousands of years. An empire is a nation that controls many territories. The Roman Empire spanned 3 continents in the first century. In the 12th century, the Mongols ruled most of Europe and Asia.

The 1500s brought a different age of empires. New technology allowed ships to travel across oceans. Europeans began traveling to distant lands. They claimed the land for themselves. They took control of it. They set up colonies. They did this even though people already lived there. This is called **colonialism**.

Spain and Portugal were the first to colonize land overseas. England, France, and the Netherlands followed. Japan and the United States later colonized land too.

THE DECOLONIZATION MOVEMENT

Decolonization is the undoing of colonialism. As colonies grew, they became difficult to control. They wanted independence from European rule. The United States was first. It broke free of British rule in 1776. This was part of the Revolutionary War (1775–1783). This action encouraged other parts of the Americas to follow.

Decolonization continued in the 20th century. Asia and Africa followed. Three dozen new states in Asia and Africa achieved independence.

A FREE PEOPLE

Not all independence is about freedom from a colonial empire. Some people celebrate freedom from an unjust government. They fight for equal representation. They fight for better leadership. The people rise up. They fight back. When they win, they celebrate their victory. They celebrate their independence.

THE FOURTH OF JULY is also known as Independence Day. It commemorates the signing of the Declaration of Independence. This document declared America's independence from British rule.

Chapter 1

Fourth of July in the United States

"What do you think?"

Amir's father stands in front of his family. He is wearing a top hat and a fake white beard. His clothing looks like the American flag.

"Do I look **patriotic**? "he asks. "Does my costume scream, 'I love America'?"

"Quite loudly," says Amir's mother.

"It's Uncle Sam," Father replies. "It's supposed to be loudly patriotic. It's for the parade. Amir and I will match!"

Last year, Amir's family watched the Fourth of July parade. This year, they are going to be in it. It was Father's idea. This year, they became American **citizens**. A citizen is an official member of a country. Father wanted to celebrate.

Amir's outfit is like his father's—without the beard. It itched too much. Amir's little sister is dressed like the Statue of Liberty.

The town is decorated for the Fourth. Red, white, and blue banners hang on the storefronts. These are the colors of the American flag. They are patriotic colors.

The streets are lined with people. Many are dressed in red, white, and blue. Some wave small American flags. Amir waves to them as he passes. His family is walking with a law group. They helped Amir's family become citizens. In front of them is a marching band. Its members play patriotic songs. The morning sun reflects off their brass instruments. Their bodies move at the same time. Each step is in sync.

In the afternoon, Amir's family attends a neighborhood barbecue. Father is wearing shorts now. His white beard is gone. Mother seems relieved.

Neighbors sit in lawn chairs. They eat hot dogs and hamburgers. They munch on potato salad. Amir's sister eats a slice of watermelon. It is bigger than her head!

Children chase one another with sparklers. Amir's neighbor is setting off small fireworks. He aims them away from the crowd. They whiz through the air. They pop and crackle.

The sun has gone down. It is time for the town's fireworks display. The show can be seen from a nearby hill. Neighbors

DID YOU KNOW?

"Uncle Sam" is a nickname for the United States. The name is linked to Samuel Wilson. He supplied beef during the War of 1812 (1812–1814). He stamped the barrels with "U.S." for "United States." Soldiers called the barrels of beef "Uncle Sams." Thomas Nast later drew an image of Uncle Sam. Nast was a political cartoonist.

bring their lawn chairs. Others bring blankets. They carry coolers with drinks.

Amir and his family spread a blanket on the grass. They watch the dark sky. They wait for the show to begin. Mother has brought more sparklers. She shares them with neighbors. Aisha has a sparkler too. She uses it to write her name in the air.

The first firework explodes with a boom. It blossoms like a blue flower. More fireworks follow. The sky looks like a magical garden.

India's **INDEPENDENCE DAY** is celebrated on August 15. This day commemorates the end of British rule in 1947. It is also when India and Pakistan became 2 nations. It is 1 of 3 national holidays in India.

CHAPTER 2

Independence Day in India

It is the eve of Independence Day. Fatima and her family gather around the television. She tells her brother to be quiet. The president is addressing the nation. She is wearing an orange, green, and white sari. These are patriotic colors. The Indian **tricolor** is behind her. This is another name for the Indian flag.

The president praises India's **democracy**. A democracy is run by an elected government. The president celebrates equality. She reminds them of their struggle for independence. She honors Mahatma Gandhi. Gandhi led the fight for independence. He used peaceful methods. Finally, the president tells of India's accomplishments. She looks forward to the future.

Fatima turns off the TV. Tomorrow is a big day. She drifts to sleep thinking about the president's words.

The Red Fort was completed in 1648. It was home to emperors.

It is a hot summer morning in New Delhi. Fatima is going to Red Fort. At this ancient site, she will watch the prime minister raise the tricolor. She has only seen it on television.

India's first prime minister raised the flag at Red Fort in 1947. It has been an Independence Day tradition ever since.

The prime minister also gives a speech. Afterward, the national anthem plays. Fatima sings along to "Jana Gana Mana."

After the anthem, there is a military parade. Each of the military branches are represented. They are wearing different uniforms. Yet they all march as one. A military band marches with them.

"Did you enjoy the ceremony?" asks Fatima's mother.

Fatima nods. "Thank you for bringing me," she says. Delhi is filled with cultural programs on this day. This was the event Fatima most wanted to see.

Fatima's brother Zahir squirms. He is eager to go home and fly kites. The sky is already thick with them.

The streets are filled with the excitement of Independence Day. Strings of lights hang from government buildings. Tricolors are displayed everywhere. Cars display the flag. Even people are wearing the tricolor.

Kites of every kind soar through the sky. The most popular kind is the tricolor. People are outside on their terraces. Someone is playing Bollywood music through a large speaker. It creates a fun atmosphere.

GO BACK, SIMON!

In 1927, the Simon Commission formed. It was made up of 7 British lawmakers. Their job was to check on the government in India. Many Indians protested. They wrote, “Go Back, Simon” on kites. They flew them throughout India. The skies were filled with the message. After that, kite flying became a form of protest.

Today, kite flying is a popular tradition on Independence Day. It is a symbol of freedom.

When they get home, Father has set out a food table. Mother has prepared a variety of tricolor dishes. Eating tricolor food is a patriotic tradition. There are traditional Indian dishes too.

Zahir holds an orange, green, and white cookie in his teeth. He steers his kite over the rooftops. It seems everyone in Delhi is doing the same. It is Fatima's favorite part of the day. The big city of Delhi seems to shrink. All the lines that divide people fade. There is no color, class, or religion. Today, there is only India.

FREEDOM DAY is celebrated on April 27. On April 27, 1994, South Africa held its first non-racial election. Nelson Mandela became president. Before 1994, a White **minority** controlled South Africa. This means there were fewer White people than Black. Despite this, Black South Africans could not vote. They could not hold office.

Chapter 3

Freedom Day in South Africa

Mama tells the story again. She tells it every Freedom Day. She was only a child when **apartheid** ended. Apartheid means separateness. Black and White South Africans were kept separate. They were treated differently. Apartheid was a form of legal racism. Nelson Mandela fought to end it.

Yinka loves the way Mama tells the story. She recalls the dark days of apartheid. Her voice is serious.

"But Mandela would not be silent," she says. "They put him in jail for 27 years. They treated him harshly. Still, they could not break him."

Yinka is full of questions, but she does not interrupt. She waits to hear what happens. At last, Mama comes to April 27. It is the best part of the story. Mama's face brightens. Her voice turns hopeful. "That was the day South Africa became free."

"Hurry up, Yinka," Mama calls. "I do not want to miss the ferry."

Mama is taking Yinka to Robben Island. It is where Nelson Mandela was imprisoned. The prison is a museum now. Freedom Day is a time to learn. It is a time to remember. Apartheid was not so long ago. Many people visit historical sites. They go to museums and cultural events. They learn about South African history.

"They sentenced Mandela to life," the tour guide explains. "He was allowed 1 visitor a year, for 30 minutes. He could send only 2 letters."

"For 27 years?"

The guide nodded.

Mandela's cell is small and lonely. Yinka cannot imagine spending 27 years there.

Freedom Day is also a time to celebrate. It is a public holiday in South Africa. Yinka has the day off from school. Mama does not have to work. The Zuma family has invited Yinka and her mother to a *braai*. It is a South African barbecue. Yinka's mother brings "chop and dop" to share. That's meat and drinks. It is **customary** at a braai. This means it is usually done.

Many guests are crowded around the television. They are watching rugby. Rugby is a popular sport in South Africa. People often watch rugby on Freedom Day. It is a way to come together.

ONE TEAM, ONE COUNTRY

In 1995, the South African rugby team beat its archrival, New Zealand. Archrivals are opponents who are very competitive with each other. It was the first big sporting event since apartheid ended. Nelson Mandela used the match to bring South Africans together. He used the slogan, "One team, one country."

BASTILLE DAY is also called *la fête nationale.* This means National Day. It falls on July 14. The Bastille was a fortress built in the 1300s. It later became a state prison. On July 14, 1789, a mob stormed the Bastille. They released the 7 prisoners held there. This marked the beginning of the French Revolution (1789–1799).

Chapter 4

Bastille Day in France

It is the eve of Bastille Day. This afternoon, Hugo watches the firefighters move the trucks. They park them on nearby streets. They are making room in the courtyard. This evening is the Firemen's Ball.

Every year, the Paris Fire Brigade throws a massive party. Firehouses across Paris open their doors to the public. It is a Bastille Day tradition.

Hugo and his parents wait in a long line. It is filled with people of all ages. Hugo is restless.

"Be patient," says Papa. "It will be worth the wait."

He is right. A huge festival takes place inside. There is music, dancing, and lots of food.

"La Marseillaise" begins to play. The crowd sings along to the national anthem.

Mama and Papa have planned a whole day in the city. The military parade begins at 10 a.m. The Avenue des Champs-Élysées is packed with people. Hugo pushes for a space up front.

An air show kicks off the celebration. Military jets soar overhead. They leave trails of red, white, and blue smoke. These are the colors of the French flag. They are patriotic colors.

The president waves to the crowd. A military band follows. It plays the national anthem. This year, the British troops appear first. It is tradition for France's **allies** to march. An ally is a friendly nation.

DID YOU KNOW?

The first Firemen's Ball took place in 1937. It wasn't planned. The firefighters had just marched in the Bastille Day parade. Local residents followed them back to the fire station. The firefighters invited them inside. They continued their celebration inside the firehouse. After that, the Firemen's Ball became a Bastille Day tradition.

The Calvary Regiment of the French Republican Guard marches in the Bastille Day parade.

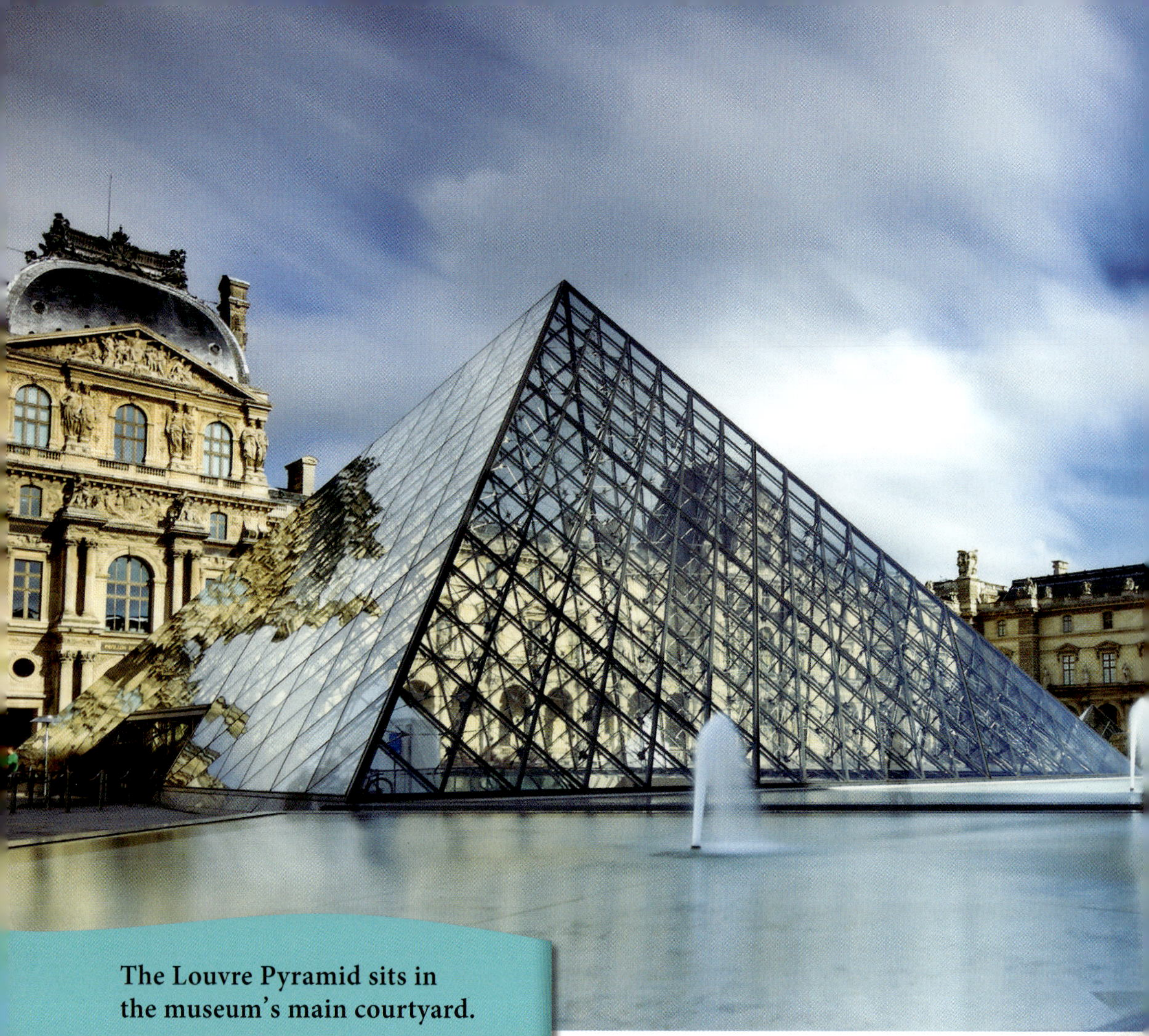

The Louvre Pyramid sits in the museum's main courtyard.

After the parade, Hugo visits the Louvre. The famous Paris museum is free on Bastille Day. Hugo strolls through famous works of art. He sees the *Mona Lisa*. The painting is actually quite small. Hugo is surprised. It is only 21 inches (53 centimeters) wide!

The sun has set. Hugo's day ends at the Eiffel Tower. The national orchestra plays classical music. The concert is free. Hugo's family spreads their picnic on the Champ-de-Mars. This is a grassy area in front of the Eiffel Tower. They share cheese and fresh bread.

The day ends with a fireworks display. The Eiffel Tower glows electric blue. Then the whole tower begins to twinkle. The crowd holds their breath. BOOM! The fireworks seem to shoot out of the tower itself. The sparks twist and spiral around the tower. They explode in time with lively music. The show lasts a half hour. What an amazing Bastille Day **finale**! A finale is an end.

The Eiffel Tower was built in 1889.

FAST FACTS: U.S. INDEPENDENCE DAY TIMELINE

July 8, 1776: First celebration took place in Philadelphia. Leaders called people by ringing the Liberty Bell. They read the Declaration of Independence for the first time.

July 3, 1781: Massachusetts makes the Fourth of July an official holiday.

July 4, 1801: The White House holds its first Fourth of July party.

1938: Congress makes the Fourth of July a federal holiday.

July 4, 1960: The current 50-star flag is revealed. It includes the newest states of Hawaii and Alaska.

LEARN MORE

BOOKS:

Anderson, Corey. *Namaste, India.* Ann Arbor, MI: Cherry Lake Publishing, 2020.

Loh-Hagan, Virginia. *American Colonies.* Ann Arbor, MI: 45th Parallel Press, 2021.

Loh-Hagan, Virginia. *The French Revolution.* Ann Arbor, MI: 45th Parallel Press, 2021.

Stokes, Floyd. *The Story of Nelson Mandela: An Inspiring Biography for Young Readers.* New York, NY: Rockridge Press, 2021.

ONLINE:

With an adult, explore more online with these suggested searches.

- Fireworks light up the Eiffel Tower on Bastille Day, Reuters via YouTube
- Indian president Droupadi Murmu's Independence Day address, Indian Express via YouTube
- Listen to "Jana Gana Mana," Soundcloud
- Listen to "La Marseillaise," a federal Soundcloud
- Listen to the "Star Spangled Banner," Soundcloud

GLOSSARY

allies (AA-liez) nations united for a common purpose

apartheid (uh-PAHR-tyte) South Africa's racist former policy of keeping Black and White people separate

citizens (SIH-tuh-zuhnz) people who owe loyalty to a government and receive protection from it

colonialism (kuh-LOH-nee-uh-lih-zuhm) government system in which one nation takes over and rules another

commemorate (kuh-MEH-muh-RAYT) to mark by a ceremony

customary (KUH-stuh-mair-ee) commonly practiced

decolonization (dee-kah-luh-nuh-ZAY-shuhn) the process of undoing a colonial government

democracy (dih-MAH-kruh-see) a government where people elect their own leaders

empire (EM-pyr) a nation that controls many territories

finale (fuh-NAA-lee) the ending of a performance

minority (muh-NOR-uh-tee) the smaller of 2 groups of people

patriotic (pay-tree-AH-tik) describing the love of one's country

sovereign (SAH-vruhn) politically independent

tricolor (TRIE-kuh-luhr) a flag having 3 colors

INDEX

ABOUT THE AUTHOR

Jennifer Kleiman has worked in educational publishing for more than 20 years. Today, she is a busy writer and editor, working on her second novel. She lives in Chicago, in a rickety old house, with her wife, 2 cats, a dog named Helen, and a yard full of chickens.